MW01234069

Brother Fire

Brother Fire

POEMS

BY W. S. DI PIERO

Alfred A. Knopf New York 2004

THIS IS A BORZOI BOOK
PUBLISHED BY ALFRED A. KNOPF

Knopf, Borzoi Books and the colophon are
registered trademarks of Random House, Inc.

Library of Congress Cataloging-in-Publication Data
Di Piero, W. S.
Brother Fire : poems / by W. S. Di Piero.—1st ed.
p.   cm.
ISBN 1-4000-4203-8
1. Religious poetry, American.
2. Erotic poetry, American. I. Title.
PS3554.I65B76 2004
811'.54—dc22   2004040915

Manufactured in the United States of America
First Edition

To Harry Grabenstein

Praise to Thee, my Lord, for Brother Fire,
by whom Thou lightest the night.
He is beautiful and pleasant,
forceful and strong.

> —St. Francis of Assisi, "Canticle of the Sun"

The meat will inherit the earth.

> —heard on a streetcar

CONTENTS

Brother Fire

Brother Francis to Brother Leone

In my dream I watched it
from a windowsill *Come see this*
raptor's shadow hushed
down green-brick tenements
Bulk beak and feather struck
and tumbled aslant the air
with sparrow or chimney swift
Wilderness breathes wherever
we are and headed to O'Hare
late fall I saw on its vague
bare branch a goshawk
grace yes and auspicious terror
I should watch with him
I should be poorer than
any wing of the air

If you could have seen
(this is a different story)
above us cloud studies
out of Constable
Pescadero's sandstone cliffs
steeped and chewed by tides
I held Brother Antonio's hand
so afraid was he the cliff
would crumble *What was that?*
as if what then came had
already happened the osprey's
sea-foam breast
sign we said of the Holy Spirit
pounding the wind

Lift and save us it stormed
up beneath our feet
Alone in Inverness
I saw a kestrel stop
in the blue and stoop
and icy blowtorch points
pecked my hands and feet
blood frothed from my side

Closer now my minders
watch and bear with me
while I'm walking barefoot
through a Tucson suburb
mesquite and prickly pear
a young peregrine
surveils me from the eye
of midmorning's sun
Last night Easter Saturday
I saw a deer enter
a bare-chested Yaqui ancient
who obeyed the dance
danced through him the poor
we think aren't with us
everywhere the deer-dancer's
concrete ramada beside the freeway
and reservation projects

Brother Ash
the less I become of what
God made me the more real

I am in His heart
Let durable goods be ashes
to pour on our heads
Brother Wing
keep me in my place
on lower Market Street
with that bare-chested man
bird of beautiful want
speechifying clothed
in chaps rat-food blanket
and cherry running shoes
Lady Poverty at his side

I walked Avenue A
knee-deep in crows spirits
of murderers and suicides
croaking *Whatever's given*
I'll take away
Drenched in a Jersey storm
I tried to send my spirit
to God my core my sphere
I asked the hawk *Who are you?*
but in some nameless place
doubled-up overcoats pushed
oxcarts past me through mud
and hungry gray children
ate their cardboard name tags
Keep and bless such images
of our own killing kind?
Buzzards slice the silence

over our heads waiting
for us their food song
How little it takes to complete
a world to find what suffices
To Brother Fire I offer
our endless poor-men's wars
our starved ruined planet
song of thrush and whitethroat
beaks of meaningless fire
piercing our hands and feet
and offer wealth to Brother Ash
and waste of blood to Brother Rag.

All in One Day

Fat crows chop from leafless elms
and sail like shadows across my window,
nervous souls backlit by a reddish sky
full of snow that hasn't fallen yet.
Waxwings passed last month
to stuff their crops with holly berries.
Starlings cry from wires . . .

    Today's news says
a dark, unworldly matter makes up
the universe we call ours, passes through
everything, leaving no trace, we're drenched
with energy that blows stars apart
and farther from us speeds explosions
I see in dreams, like last night—
each time I named a constellation
it became another.

    On a day like this,
crows budding on the crabby oaks,
the blood ghosts I see in human forms
could be a necessary fantasy
of nerve cells, dopamine, or appetite,
bodies modeled from phantom fluids,
passing through a world that doesn't exist,
or exists in the mind of God.

    I thought the child
hooting at a ruff of fallen leaves
would shovel them at me like a war
or bridal game, but the armfuls scooped
above her head rattled down,
wrinkled flames on her shoulders,

and she tested its atomized perfume,
clapping her orange mittens, fall's
first child, hollering
  Come down here, you!
That's when I felt most alive
inside matter's reechy stuff,
unseen, intensely real.
Later, riding into town,
held and rocked by the L's steelworks,
from my seat I saw the season crouch
behind the platform, and a college girl,
pigeon-toed and pale,
  standing there
in bawling November, rails and gravel
moonlit like snow, the world's freaked bark
scraped to pith, an express blowing through
whipped leaves around her feet . . .
Our mud-flake life, and rain sheets,
contracting to a brown glassy drop
that clung to her reddening hair.

The Fifties

We trained for it at school,
to duck for cover, arms
over head, crouched
tight to wall or stoop
when Wednesday's sirens rang,
or under an iron-hoofed desk,
holding our leaky breath
until an all clear sounded
or the light storm struck,
as it did each week before
Howdy Doody time.
Family of four,
all smiles over supper,
in the unsteady screen
of primitive TV.
Outside, a siren blows,
each elevates from a chair
and floats to a corner
like a planet in its ring,
until the okay comes
or the new mock solar wind
shreds china, pitchers, drapes,
weightless forks and flowers
creaming the air, and we,
thank God unhurt, tune in
for Civil Air assistance.
Tonight, from the newsroom,
came the same kind of seedy
light, but instead of supper
(not to make too much

of this) a video clip
drizzled a fish-eye view:
L-shaped counter, shelves,
cookies, jerky, soup,
then, in flannel shirts,
watchcaps sleeved down
like Hittite helms, "two youths,"
jabbing what seem like guns
at an Asian clerk who,
now visible to us,
smears in nuclear wind
and falls out of the frame.

"Standing Man and Sun"

At eye level off
to the edge of sight
I keep close to me
this gray postcard:
rifled lines, a plain
from which grows "Man,"
weedy, scrawny-boned,
big generic hands,
head fibered from
the raven energy
of big feet and trunk.
Nothing natural.

I need and love
its opera of essentials.
Ground. Sun. Stalk.
To see, to be. The sky's there
because a sun shines in it,
shineless. I want to keep
the shadow late sunlight
franks on the table, this gray
unstable print of me,
memento, darkening
with time, gauntly complete,
lightly penciled on this plain.

A View of the Studio

My train that early evening
ran toward its tunnel,
a gray nothing, I thought,
waiting beyond. Daylight
shed its scales, hamlets of lights
pumped from hillsides, trackside
TV emanations wiped past,
aluminum greens and blues,
instant to instant, identically
sized, the world plying form
on form, revising itself
as I watched. Headlights
mashed rockface, vineyards
troweled my window, then meadows,
runoff acidic pouchings,
and marbled wind raking
clouds into sea-motion
minerals, veils dragged
past my view until
the landscape sheared off
into combed cobalt blues
channeled into the mountain,
where graffiti fragments knifed
like blue ice and deranged
the scene. The windows
held our faces close
to shadow grids masked
by rent disclosures,
this fresh infinitude
of line and volume.

When we emerged, the small
village station lay
among its dark mountains
in a casual perfection
of night snow scooped by wind.
The more snow covered tracks,
switching lights, platform, roofs,
the more it revealed red
umbrellas, violet coats,
porters' wagons and clock,
a silent place sedated
in its changes, and I
felt delivered, unfinished,
to bright and solid scenes
melting through me as I
streamed helpless into them.

Dancing on New Year's Eve at Dave and Sheila's

"Everybody's looking for something"
and everything smells good.
My sweating partner's hips
push harder into mine,
tequila yeasting through our skin
and we'd lick each other dry,
drink more, do it again
while blue lamps twitch
between the others lost,
until someone at midnight
kills the music, calls us
to the front door where we grab
and kiss whoever's near,
squeezed out into the night
where woolly pops like corks
or muffled distant gunshots
are gunshots in fact, high times,
bullets to the stars.
They won't fall to earth here
where in June mysterious
citron lilies bloom, a perfume
more intense than lemons.
How did they get here?
Eyewitness News tells us
what guns cost beyond
the freeway. We smell ourselves,
the grand cedar by the door,
peanuts, booze, and sweat.
How can we not love them?
When the music snaps on again,

we weave back to the floor
adrift in each other's arms,
and love it more, that constancy
of beat and song,
she presses her mouth
to my ear, rubs harder with me
and sings We're here because
we're here because we're here.

Mowers

Untended two months in my absence,
our backyard's pigweed and razorgrass
stood waist high against my Weed Eater's
murderous blade. I bent, off balance,
and scythed tight crescents, mowing with
no plan—that night I'd dream it nicked
my shin and hummed into the air
bone-dust and blood. The dying plants lay
in loose, soft loaves, like sleepers
holding close against night fear or wind.
She who let them grow, preoccupied with us,
house, far dying parents—one remembers
childhood German and "meadowlark"
but not his daughter's name; the ethereal other
recalls what bountiful future waits—
stood a safe distance behind, her voice
wired to the keening edge as gnats
and damselflies fluttered from my cuts.
Wanting worse while she tied off sheaves,
I slanted down to hack and kick up dirt
and stones that scattershot my face, wanting
to take something, everything, to its end,
right where our weed garden thrived
with wild fennel and iris. It took two days
and left us weeping and depleted
in our cozy hamlet of shattered steeples,
windfall fences, and stubbled churchyards
where green stuff was already growing back.

The View from Here

It's not hard to find them any night, sleeping under autumn stars,
the nameless, swept away or under, dozy, maybe asleep, car heater off,
a gentle poisoned wind blowing through the window, the toddler
kicks and growls like a dog dreaming, the older son's closed eyes
twitch as if he can't chase or flee those pictures fast enough,
and the parents, too big and hot, how every hour or so they wake,
touch, nudge to make room in their early-model front seat,
fresh water to last the night, chips and Snickers, diapers, gum,
celebrity gossip rags, cover sheets for the children,
breathing inside sullen steel blued by moonlight, under a trestle
or interstate, in an off-season stadium lot, untended campground
or back street, or parked there behind a strip mall's Dumpster pod,
just like last night, times before and to come, if we look to see,
then to imagine the tribes together, hundreds of junkers like tortoises,
in an abandoned drive-in, windows steamy, voices and grunts
as we walk past the secrets of the day-jobbers, housecleaners,
nannies, pickers, and busboys camouflaged among us, on their way
to greater goods, dreaming of how we stand here watching them.

The Girl Found in the Woods

She planned it to perfection,
studied to fall a certain way,
the correct distance tree limb
to ground, as if in consciousness
she rehearsed the completed scene
she'd live into, a string of pictures
in her suburban remoteness,
the drop measured and tested
like any nuance of despair,
the day cool, pressured by headwinds
she bent her body through,
biking miles from town to locate
this place nobody would find,
to the live oak she hangs from
observed by lesser birch and gum,
while her natural self told friends
she needed time (*Whatever you do,*
don't worry) alone, to ride the hills
she loved. And so she disappeared
into whatever sound her heart
flushed through her head and spared
others the shame of finding her.
In that silence, after she stepped
or jumped, or slipped, and the bough
creaked from the sudden flight
of weight, the clearing ticked
with ground squirrel, coyote, deer
who walked past pictures training
across their eyes. Rock, bush,
tree branch, mistletoe.

Increased Security

Venus, demure tonight, as always, sharp
in my western sky which flops each time
the Fourth of July's sheet-lightning fireworks
blow from the eastern side of town, hooping
embarcadero lights, black bay and bridge,
star light, star bright, seer, solid and chaste
in her infinitude, calmly waiting
to watch the oceans buckle, cities burn,
while Catherine wheels and maypole pom-poms mock
her constancy, far-off sugared surprises
flaring orderly reds and purpled blues
above the silent pod of black-and-whites
and fireboats, fighter jets cruising,
chopper beams fingering the crowd
I can't see here, don't need to see to know
that while kids sing a jingling brass-band march,
be kind to your web-footed friends
for a duck may be somebody's mother,
the sky shrieks at Venus, mother of all,
who watches from her distance, hears booms
and alarmed whistles over the heads of mothers
who squeeze their children's hands, fathers boosting
sons and daughters up onto their shoulders,
the better for them to catch the air, for balance,
still grabbing at the artificial fires
we all look up to, while we wait for more.

———————

"How Do I Get There?"

Make the first left
then follow your headlights
chasing all those leaves
out West River Drive
so full of increase late
fall maples and oaks
drive past Boathouse Row
and the Schuylkill on your right
past the dead power station
and greatly gilt Joan of Arc
riding Franklin Parkway
to liberate the museum
so don't forget to salute
Rubens and the rest
ignoring riverside lights
spooled inside the water
and shrunken freeway ramps
night traffic creases
bear right at City Hall
more leaves newspapers
butterflies in taillights
then take Broad Street south
go go until it's all
brickfronts and corner stores
right again on Wolf
watch for the wilder kids
playing after dark
check your mirrors lock
your doors now everything waits
listens for you while you pass

Baldini's funeral home
where more than ever the air's
a gasp of running leaves
that crackle under your tires
so follow them until
they grab the marbled steps
and then you'll know you're there.

—*for J. T. Barbarese*

Somehow They Got Three Stories Up

the brownstone warehouse roof
to spray-paint their hammy
urgent script corner to corner
where bridge traffic has to look
the telemarketer just laid off
the aggrieved low-rider posting
a cigarette in his girlfriend's mouth
welders receptionists minimum-wagers
business suits in empty vans
all bypassing NARCOVEGAN
senseless with a bite of sense
we're not meant to understand
They got exactly what they wanted
I made you look you dirty crook
I stole your mother's pocketbook
I turned it in I turned it out
I turned it into sauerkraut
They must have scaled down
in window-washer harnesses
fluked the word across that grime
then flipped and dangled like bats
to study the city upside down
a dark blue lake and in that lake
a white cuticle and starry
bioluminescent fish
the lake surface spiked by flattop
towers wigged with black concrete
and headlights' molecular strands
more vexing messages.

Glenn Miller and His Orchestra

These two young immortals
practicing Lindy Hop
the bandshell empty
her bare feet and tights
his treaded huaraches
churched by all that concrete
where yesterday the city's
brass band lofted
"King Cotton" and "Muskrat Ramble"
silent now except for this
narrow-waisted wind
in the concourse's pollard
plane trees and poplars
two and kick watched by
empty chairs and turn
and three and grave-park quiet
hooped in their arms
like classic calligraphy's
perfect circle
completed in one stroke
Sunday's wonder of
repeated miscued steps
and softened clap when
she palms his hand
spins into her laughter
and now ladies and gentlemen.

Brass Earrings

I found these
The dry-cleaning clerk

looked nothing
and too much like you

in your pocket
Fake antiqued

hammered coins
from nowhere I remember

incised with cobras and lightning
Nice jacket

My bearish mothballed loden
fatigued in its plastic wrap

a great buy years ago
with someone else

They can't be hers
despite this vague

old-flame's aura
and they're not yours

though I'd have given them
to you if you stayed

The fishhook stems
meaninglessly crossed

the "Prosperity" girl's
shiny not yet hatched

lifeline
They're really pretty

Tonight don't ask why
the creaky snow's voice

keeps changing first hers
back then who talked

into my collar
then yours no longer here

and now my smiling
lifeline seamstress

I'll let you keep them
Someone's scuffed Roman

cheapies lost and found
then lost again right now.

Ghetto Nuovo

Water lights quaking under
the blocked ironwork bridge

spindrifted up scabby walls
like selves we might have been

Rosettes and meaningless
Pre-Raphaelite lunettes

panties drying on lines
voices from balconies

we couldn't even see
chromatic with our own

too much likeness but
never quite enough

We weren't waiting
for anything to happen

We noted the small lion's
head wrought into the arch

those buttoned-up sentry boxes
we couldn't reach just as

we didn't know what we had
and maybe laughed too hard

at lingerie and spirits
flying up the walls.

Sometime Nights

Sweetest meat
close to the bone

commonplaces
things known

pronouncements
come be my love

take it or leave it
get here you

old facts
flesh rags

the morning fog's
shorn whitecaps

I touch your
damp hair spooned

on the pillow
salt and meat

we two negatives
on windowpanes

How you sway
in our burly air

your slow way
tights first

bra blouse skirt
pinned-up hair

bracelet rings
full-size mirror

check everything
make sure you're there.

On the Island

Far enough to hear
not see it I climbed
where fat boulder track
narrowed to ginger trees
shadow roots brush
monkeypod mynahs
falling branch to branch
things coming into what
they are a stream I barely
saw behind the trees
shredded stones and mud
through a purple dark

To balance myself to breathe
I grabbed a darker mass
of spined oily leaves
and slipped on creamed
guava-blossom flesh
dropping everywhere
in answer to the water
that cracked stones with sounds
lost before they're thought
and the unassuming stream
broke into view as I fell
into grave pulp and skins

the cataract's small sound
a hiss I can still hear
waiting up ahead
if I got that far

and made the loud falls
I never did see while
smells of sweet dead plenty
that upset and held me
make me sicker now
whenever I breathe fumes
of any current bearing
fruit too ripe to eat.

What Is This

repeating mental image
cobbled street
close-grained sky
limestone archways
sunny hill town
I've never visited
but recognize it's
where I came from
that found a life in me

The incline flattens to
an alpine house a home
in my nerves an empty
street here I feel more
of the image than in it
still making my way
across uneven stones
and won't reach the top
until I stop wanting to

In an antiquary's postcard
shoebox I knew I'd find
something I didn't know
I needed and happened
on a photograph by
Gustave Eugenio Chauffourier
"about whom little is known"
whose image replicates
my steep phantom town

Same wooden shutters
loping arches light-
embossed cobblestones
an added element this
smudged village girl
bell-jar smock and apron
halfway up my hill
who will offer me
well water from that jar

the scene veiled somehow
by sand and fluid pearl
I know I've been here too
and felt crushed shell
shifting in my heart
inside image life
vagrant still doubtful
promise of what's there
in a lost unknown place.

Blue Moon

—OCTOBER 31, 2001

They're gathering now
cone-head ghouls Spider-Man
fly-by-nighters' burnt-cork cheeks
flailed sheets and twiggy voices
Mama stalking a border dog's
crescent around back around
as if to fend off certain harm
October's second sodium moon
basting the street and barbecue ribs
and links she smoked all day
to keep her four boys close
no begging door-to-door not
with new monsters wakened
Anything can happen here
tonight unlike past years free
to knock and shriek
now they spook themselves
overdub hip-hop shouts going
nowhere fast these fearless fat
boys past whom skip fuzzy whelps
tittering mice and bunnies clamped
to adults who keel them house
to house and now I see them
as a broken flock of dispersed
wild children wandering
adults and myself among them
like medieval gangs of the blind

the destitute the deranged the lost
beyond our ranks of city lights
to beg and thumb our way
suburb to rail tracks to hills
across lunar stubble fields.

A Man of Indeterminate Age on Subway Grate

The city loves inside my head

    In the morning fever all through the night

The city lives inside my head

    I got steam heat I got

Do not remove this person

    I am of the Holy Spirit see us rise

I am the police I am loving

    Inside garment trucks my ears brains what have you

Who feels what I hear in my mouth

    Running shoes pumps wing tips sandals stilettos

I think I have a bone in my stomach

    Here hey how did I get here

I'm the body of the city and immense with subways

    And if you should survive to one hundred and five

Floating up here that howl down there is me

Of our time invisible angel

Of castoffs replays tax frauds lost lease sales

Roaring steel wings hover above to take us

Cigarette holder

It wigs me.

Two Stops

14TH STREET

You handsome you
keep crooning
into your cell
that low sweet
downtown rag
or blues line
strange strungalong
Chinese pitches
bouncing to
whoever's there
Say what you mean
Run up minutes
singing tart
intensities
while they last
to satellites
near the moon.

86TH STREET

Your cheek O my
brunette three panes
away its purple
half-mask maybe
the station's sooty
lighting or shadow of

someone's paper
but forsythia
along drives
softball fields and
shale outcrops
blooms down at us
who are the horizon
we sit or stand on
until the doors shut
and flicker you
the opposite way.

The Birthmark

How could this pregnant high-
schooler chewing oat bran
know she's already minted
her unborn with wine stain
hairy mole or harelip when
she stilts head on hands
her fingers or palm pressing
her face the fetal face
It's like a hot-iron touch
the elder women say
that sears something lasting
into the unborn's skin
who grows from this moment
marked for life by too much
cruel passionate belief
though the mother slaps
her hands away as if
she could stop it in time.

Red Sandals

Finely tinted matter
to fill the outline of shin
and arch and her letter
We want to complete
creation with desire
blunt feet that stretch
one by one from behind
the door feeling for
her shoes as if to test
a temperature toes
stretched into the saddle
catching for a moment
in the cowhide weave
her hand so matter-of-fact
as it pulls on ankle straps
that chafe the aroused
spur of skin on bone
a small forgotten pain
alive again and glowing
happiness from which
the rest of her rises.

Didn't You Say Desire Is

like the elephant fog
shredded north
a white sun going down
Bessemers fired
through clouds horizoned
on my dog-eared stack
It feels good and right
to waste earnest hours
of an early evening's
daylight saving time
in uncertainty and want
these cranky climates
changing in us while we
haven't started dinner yet.

The Sky-Blue Chair

Its wide-grain gravel rooftop
one street over from mine
like but not like enough
beach beige and gray
Wildwood-by-the-Sea
where in such a chair
I dozed on such a beach
clouds worked out above me
voices trawled the surf
I was alone with the world
disappearing into
chafing ruddy vapors
I've never seen anyone
yet some days it's tipped
or skewed by wind or body
I must have missed
its polymer blueness
my Jersey afternoon
of celestial beach reading
(Freddy and the Space Ship)
overhead a single-
prop thrashing a banner
What good is it if no one
even flops or sunbathes
on that blue hinge holding
time and space together
even when summer fog
squalls its happy presence
into oblivion for now
azure sea-surface

to black sea canyons
Friends ask does anyone
ever sunbathe nude
or read a book do they
see you and stare back
Not ever not yet although
sometimes I think I see
on the sand-blown roof
on the sky's blue screen
a carnal memory
a body maybe mine.

Suzanne on the Sofa

How it was for her
I didn't know then
or why she insisted
in the swarming parlor
we dance like Greeks
next to the pink punch
What seemed most
hers that night
wasn't really there
She outkicked men
lined up both sides
of her diminished form
stooping lower than us
hooted when she rose
a happiness more like
explosive grievance
at that winter party
snow fallen outside
as if just then grown
upon the windowsill
and of her finger made
a Popsicle she sucked clean
outdrank other girls smoked
with stifled elation gargled
sounds that identified her
loosely somewhere French
all written into the script
Her other men said the same
Who noticed it Did you
She fooled us all

unfinished nubbin thumb
as if the child she was
sucked it too long no one
noticed while she snapped
to our zither music
another finger incomplete
digits like abandoned tasks
one briefly on her other
hand briefer when she smoked
hours of talk days weeks
passed before I noticed
how she folded into
my lap biting a raw breakfast
hot dog moist pincée mouth
violet eyes yellow flaw
You can't look anywhere else
the twisted nightie showing
small-boned shoulders
one bare breast and her
throaty whimpering
merciless and meek
when I asked about her hand
opened for a cigarette
and my fumbled lighter
tocked her leg bent
under haunch and pillow
I wouldn't recognize
what it was I wanted
to eat her up and forget
the ever present wrap she said

stabilized her tricky knee
I still can't recompose
stories she kept changing
alpine accident absent
father French mother American
or vice versa *envious of*
her daughter's broken beauty
terror alone on the slopes
the prosthesis she now
began kittenish to stroke
while she stroked my leg
and jostled into French
she knew I didn't understand
kissing smoke into my mouth
on my thigh cancanning
the fatigued hot dog
and magical finger
then tapped her hollow thing
That's me too what's missing.

Ortlieb's Uptown Taproom

The sax's rayon shirt tonight fires up
flamingos, pink parrots, blue palms . . .
He trues his porkpie so the pinky diamond
winks into the smoky room. The drummer
looks beyond us all, seeing things
we don't, winged things cutting the air.
A second set at midnight, the brewery long
closed down beyond that door. After their shift,
the cookers and machinists passed through
for beers and shots, punched Bobby Darin
into the jukebox. By three a.m. they're home,
leftovers in the oven, or TV dinners,
upstairs a sea of restless candied dreaming
(roller-skating on ice, a red wet finger
in the toaster), and when he sits to eat,
he remembers waking as a child
to mountain bagpipers in his village,
Christmas morning, peasant music wheezing
high and thin down under the window.
Their goatskin bags call like animals,
the herdsmen's arms muscled like his own
checking heat and pressure gauges,
breathing a tune dreamed up as he goes along,
like our flamingo sax, in his ecstasy tonight,
who blows bagpipe music through our hearts
and the sudsy breath of drinkers quitting work.

Christopher Columbus Park

Checkers, bocce, some days rummy or hearts,
early fall under chestnut trees. Then winter,
inside the rec center, bingo and widows
while snow dazes 8th Street's traffic lights.
Summer, finally, Mikey and Sal
warm themselves in beach chairs on the grass.
Sticky sunshine, stogies, Phillies games
quacking from transistors, dago red
dispensed from crystal altar-boy cruets
going up in smoke. Some days,
in pressed T-shirts, Sal played sweet potato,
Mikey the mandolin, bald heads nodding
like tulips. Why wasn't I surprised
by its senselessness, the word we used
to justify what happened, anything
that happens, childhood friends at odds
over money, maybe, or baseball stats,
the unions or Democrats, boiling over
as usual, nose to nose, blue in the face,
until, this one time, Mikey goes home
and comes back with his old kraut Luger,
and Sal starts to run, crabby legs and arms
lacing the air, until he drops, as if life
were one short breath held and spent,
while the pistol rabbits into the air
from slow-motion Mikey's hand,
who can't think fast enough to feel
his own heart failing him. Their cronies
couldn't help. What was the fight about?
He never carried the gun. The widows said

bad blood between old fools too old to know
bad blood was there. One generation kept
the story alive, trying to make it make sense,
but it dried up and blew away, then stuck
here to me, where there's still no saying how
the angers of a place can live in us
like love, thriving, awfully our own.

Prayer Meeting

Hankies and sheets, hopeless routine longing,
my mother and I in the cellar twice each week,
her Sunbeam coasting under screws of steam,
me on my knees by the ironing board
to call Hail Marys. Our bodies vapored
into immaculate words. Shirttails talked back.
I wanted more than what I prayed for.
Her music-box antiphons mumbled us
around the decades. Neither of us knew
why or what we implored. God jerked alive
in repetitions. I reeled Him in. She must
have been appeasing me because she feared
offending Him, deity of hurt and rue,
of affliction and splintered rafters weeping
wan work dungarees, school uniforms,
all together in our separate voices.
The God of iron, unsatisfied, hissed back.

St. Agnes Infirmary

The flinty beet flavor
melted from a dream
of frisky blades and rags
that leaked into my throat
and gagged my cry. I choked
on wanting to be heard—
blood gouts like words
stuck to my lips,
tasting rank matter
set me free, the soul
I'd imagined a bright, thin disk
became my jellied meat.

It comes back to me now,
the bedroom wallpaper
sweating wolfish shadows
while rough hands wound me
in sheets of darkening blood
and fumbled me into a car.
I thrilled to winter air
passing through our Chevy
into my closing throat,
until, at St. Agnes,
white coats seared my veins
with lamps and iron tongs.

It comes in this surprising air,
on a familiar street,
through this bus window,
a chilled wind that scrapes

my lips and nostrils
like that cold ecstasy,
blood falling, my first
seasonal taste of the world,
it frees and stops my words
this afternoon when,
the leaves just turning red,
fall air blows through my head.

Evening Errand

Dimples in the dirt, the baby's blue sleepsuit, Bruno's guttural denials,
cash bundles in the closet (why didn't she ask?), under the window
the ladder built by wiry hands she must have felt like warm breath
across her throat or arm while she lay awake and he served time, unplotted
images and words in her head like weather smeared on glass.
I now think, knowing what I do, that the day I crashed into her life
she was planning another appeal, suckered by sharpies and lowlifes,
because she wanted to believe his truth, that day the half-ball bat
left my hands, propellered across the street, broke the baker's window
into beads and blades that fell, it seemed, in silence, and killed wedding cakes
waiting for their occasion. The baby's body a black husk, hands and feet
eaten by foxes, skull so thin that, like certain facts, it broke
under a policeman's pencil like a shell of frost, none of which I knew
when the baker hollered he'd sue my parents or send me to jail.
I remember her calm behind the counter (that can't be true, the glass
boomed, I think) as if waiting for a steady customer like me
who might just as well not come, and that was all the sense it made.
Twice a stowaway, immigrant like us, lying his way to the good life,
he told our Cinnamon Bun Lady truths he made himself believe.
I earned that money with my own hands. I'm not the ogre in the woods.
My aunts, telling me fifty years later, couldn't remember when
Mrs. Hauptman came among us, or if that's what she called herself,
or if it was even she, because you never know. Anyway, there she was,
minding the struffi, cannoli, and cream puffs, quiet, flour-dusty, 1955,
when in jaundiced August I lost my grip, the same year Lindy said:
"We Americans are a primitive people. We do not show discipline."
It happened and still happens all at once, a nerve bundle of facts
and the image of a stocky boy going back and forth each evening,
store to home and dinner, whistling standards, barely conscious,
shamed to thoughtlessness, chewing the heel of a ten-cent loaf.

Ten P.M. in Kezar's

The arrangement's vague at first.
Pocket doors half-open,
young hands at a piano,
vinyl-covered sofa, lamp
lighted by a sunny window,
each shifting as if uncertain
of its place, until a woman
filling out a fruity apron
beside me—*Here, big boy*—
offers a quarter-moon
from a fennel bulb.
I bite, the scene goes still,
a salty fleshiness
in my mouth.
  Now,
the woman in the apron,
the child and her étude,
and so many others gone,
something vapors from
this free brandy the barkeep
sets out, a new product,
have a taste, but I'm
about to weep for loss
over these anise hints,
so to appease myself
I offer it back to her,
who sniffs, shakes her head,
and says it must be me.

Lightning Bugs

The boy on my street whose flashlight
jacked last night across my face
shows me charred pebbles in a jar,
his mother hollering *Jo-Jo,*
where you? Time to eat.

The same cooled
simmering sparks
I once made into zinc gems
greening on my fingers
while their little glows faded,

evening dark coming down
and a purple storm ended
in women's voices yelling
Come home now or else.
I knew they wouldn't last,

those weakened souls
that came back every summer
from wherever else they go,
who visit now, in my window-
flash, a sensor house-light's

weegee when I pass,
or high beams chipping the rain,
our cinders in a jar, while stars
still burn above, just as bright
when they're already dead.

Honey

We four were fat with talk
under their fresh-painted pergola.
You giggled sounds like *blue spruce*
and *hollyhocks*, he told us how
he chicken-wired chaos
into that terraced garden,
she announced road-stand watermelon
while the smart scout did its work.

Yellow jackets write such precise
expectations on the air.
You dummied up when one,
sensing sweet melon flesh,
alighted to sample nectar
on your lips. I watched it
wanting more, wanting in
to probe your tongue,

and you watched me as if I were
someone or somewhere else.
The day before, for no reason,
"Death that hath suck't the honey
of her breath" looped in my ear,
and now came again
while we waited for the sting, or cry,
that didn't come.

Romeo's words played back
like children's nonsense rhymes
when this morning's storm drained

yellow jackets to my ligustrum tree,
its spermy scent plied with sweet broom
and lemon blossoms like those in their garden
when the wooer petted your mouth
and you smiled as if you knew
it couldn't hurt, your eye on me,
making sure we understood
you make your charms available
but don't give them away.

Maenad

—ROMAN COPY OF GREEK ORIGINAL OF
LATE FIFTH CENTURY B.C.

Before she rolls and stands,
sheets eddied in oyster shell
ridges so sharp around
the deep thighs and bent knee
I could cut myself on them,
her head on the pillow bends
to study what she's become.
I look down at her
and see antiquity,
a supplicant's chiton pleats
wilting from the torso,
the slouching god inside her
who melts her bones and shivers
through the stone, down
where ecstasy pulls us
here on the messy bed,
but instead of standing,
her body softens more
while she looks up at me.
"What are you staring at?"

A Cold June

Ice, dirt, gray miraculous flesh. I can put my finger on the space debris
burred all night on my window, until fog effaces it and other signs.
What am I looking for? This comet dust that seems to burn recalls
the cold basilica, in June, my pious friend and I invited to the altar,
the priest (sour voice, sour heart) reciting: locked in the reliquary, livid,
translucent, like a flake of trapped ash, floats a slice of Christ's heart,
it's all true, doctors testified, what looks like a dragonfly's wing
is His living blood cells. How curtly he announced it, impatient
with nonbelief before it showed itself, impatient with my indifference,
while my friend wheezed through his mouth, awed, worshipful,
and the father looked from him to me, as if to say you can't love
without astonishment, the miraculous wants innocence beyond knowledge
of contradiction, not the monocle of my unbelief. Yet now each night
the comet somehow cuts across the relic, a coincidence I can credit
because it makes no sense, to believe in what I know is not true life.
The stars and gods have made us so that we make meaning of what
resists us, and of such resistance make a consciousness, a rotund
coherence of accident and law. The imagination in one stroke
squeegees subway passages, manhole-cover steam cones, clouds,
bus wheels' blowback snow, the dance of minor things
sifting from or into others, momentously. I smudge an afterimage
on my window to mark a juicy slice of being. What happens now?
Buses and cafés explode in holy lands, in Hackensack
a father kisses his son in peace, money eats dirt on Wall Street,
Big Casino overdoses across the street, the Gypsy to the Werewolf sings
Even a man who is pure at heart and says his prayers by night
Will become a wolf when the wolfbane blooms, and the moon is full and bright.
Glacial dust wasting away across the sky where gods have come and gone,
downstairs a student's cello practices praise and questions for those gods.
Woeful, nervous, almost content, he falters and plays the phrase again.

Easter Candy

State prison, its one lame ginkgo tree,
then more each block, increasing west
on Moyamensing, with sycamores,
oaks, upholsterers, hoagie shops,
and across Broad Street, near our house,
more ginkgos gabled across the sward,
their bridal elegiac leaves
darkening grass with golden light,
while I kick through fallen ones.
Riding past in their old Chevy
in another season, the boy
itchy in the backseat's April warmth
looks out and tries to pick one object
from another, but also sees
an unnerving wash of oneness.
Father frowns. Mother sighs
and raps her beaked red fingernail
against the dash, marking time.

A voice he feels inside his gut
calls to the branches overhead
in Easter leaf, while the car pans
the Penrose Diner and Delaware,
the oil-works' cat converter flares
sunning the river's greasefire surface,
the Four Roses distillery's burnt-
plastic stench blown downriver,
then the airport, its eager planes,
Tinicum Marsh, rufous towhees,
herons mating near runways,

things of the world that offer only
what they are, then come the lawns
and perfected graves of Holy Cross,
holding all the fathers and mothers
who buried fathers and mothers, sad
Girones, Di Pieros, and all
their dialects turned soot and bone.

I'm here kicking leaves again.
The car's long gone. Cousin Al,
the Candy Man from Upper Darby,
he's gone, too. That Easter, driving
to his store, I had childish whims
that after death we would become
mobbed beings of light, free,
in happy spheres above the trees,
no falling leaves to puzzle the air,
no almonds like the shoebox full
Al offered me downstairs
     —Take
as much as you want.
     Don't say a word—
then led my pockets and me into
his sugared underground, past vats
of nougat, strawberry taffy, mixers
doing the polka in creamy tubs,
cloudy pink smocks of stout
women swaying at their stations
in hairnets and chocolate mittens,
picking and dragging hazelnuts,

jellies, raisins, walnut bits,
pulling odd sweet forms from mess . . .
How could I know that cherry and grape
burn the tongue with knowledge of
a time when sweetness can't be had,
and yet we taste them anyway
because it burns, that taste of us,
while the girls' quick, darkened hands pick
our perishable ecstasies,
and we keep working to save what we can.

The Kiss

The mossy transom light, odors of cabbage
and ancient papers, while Father Feeney
polishes an apple on his tunic.
I tell him I want the life priests have,
not how the night sky's millions
of departing stars, erased by city lights,
terrify me toward God. That some nights
I sleepwalk, curl inside the tub,
and bang awake from a dream of walking through
a night where candle beams crisscross
the sky, a movie premiere somewhere.
Where am I, Father, when I visit a life
inside or outside the one I'm in?
In our wronged world I see things
accidentally good: fishy shadows thrown
by walnut leaves, summer hammerheads
whomping fireplugs, fall air that tastes
like spring water, oranges, and iron.

"What are you running from, my dear,
at morning mass five times a week?"
He comes around the desk, its failing flowers
and Iwo Jima inkwell, holding his breviary,
its Latin mysteries a patterned noise
like blades on ice, a small-voiced poetry
or sorcery. Beautiful dreamer,
how I love you. When he leans down,

his hands rough with chalk dust
rasp my ears. "You don't have the call,"
kissing my cheek. "Find something else."

On the subway home I found
a Golgotha air of piss and smoke,
sleepy workers, Cuban missiles drooping
in their evening papers, with black people
hosed down by cops or stretched by dogs.
What was I running from? Deity flashed
on the razor a boy beside me wagged,
it stroked the hair of the nurse who waked
to kiss her rosary. I believed the wall's
filthy cracks, coming into focus
when we stopped, held stories I'd find
and tell. What are you running from,
child of what I've become?
Tell what you know now
of dreadful freshness and want,
our stunned world peopled
by shadows solidly flesh,
a silted fountain of prayer
rising in our throat.

ACKNOWLEDGMENTS

I thank the editors of the magazines in which some of these poems first appeared: *The Threepenny Review* ("Evening Errand," "On the Island," "Blue Moon"), *The Berlin Journal: A Magazine from the American Academy in Berlin* ("A Cold June," "Didn't You Say Desire Is"), *The New Criterion* ("Christopher Columbus Park," "Mowers"), *The New Yorker* ("The Kiss"), *TriQuarterly* ("All in One Day," "Increased Security"), *Poetry* ("Brother Francis to Brother Leone," "Honey," "Somehow They Got Three Stories Up"), *Slate* ("Prayer Meeting," "Ortlieb's Uptown Taproom"), *The Progressive* ("The View from Here"), and *The Cortland Review* ("Dancing on New Year's Eve at Dave and Sheila's"). "The View from the Studio" appeared in the catalog *RICHTER 848*, edited by David Breskin (The Shifting Foundation: San Francisco Museum of Modern Art, 2002). " 'How Do I Get There?' " appeared in *Living Under South Street*, a photographic essay by Jonathan Elderfield (Kehrer Verlag, 2003). Special thanks to the American Academy in Berlin for its generosity and support.

A NOTE ABOUT THE AUTHOR

W. S. Di Piero was born in South Philadelphia in 1945. He is the author of eight books of poetry, as well as four volumes of translations. He writes about art for the *San Diego Reader* and has published three collections of essays and criticism on art, literature, and personal experience. He has received a Guggenheim Fellowship, a National Endowment for the Arts grant, and a Lila Wallace–*Reader's Digest* Writers' Award. He lives in San Francisco and teaches at Stanford University.

A NOTE ON THE TYPE

The text of this book was set in a typeface called Bell. The original punches for this face were cut in 1788 by the engraver Richard Austin for the typefoundry of John Bell (1745–1831), the most outstanding typographer of his day. They are the earliest English "modern" type design, and show the influence of French copperplate engraving and the work of the Fournier and Didot families. However, the Bell face has a distinct identity of its own, and might also be classified as a delicate and refined rendering of Scotch Roman.

Composed by Creative Graphics, Allentown, Pennsylvania
Printed and bound by United Book Press, Baltimore, Maryland
Designed by Robert C. Olsson